ANTARCTICA:
THE LAST WILDERNESS

UNDERSTANDING GLOBAL ISSUES

Published by Smart Apple Media
1980 Lookout Drive
North Mankato, Minnesota 56003
USA

This book is based on *Antarctica: Protecting the Last Wilderness*
Copyright ©1995 Understanding Global Issues Ltd., Cheltenham, England

UGI Series Copyright ©2004 WEIGL PUBLISHERS INC.

Library of Congress Cataloging-in-Publication Data

Bocknek, Jonathan.
  Antarctica, the last wilderness / Jonathan Bocknek.
    v. cm. -- (Understanding global issues)
Includes bibliographical references (p.   ).
Contents: Heroes of the ice continent -- Land of extremes -- A fragile
ecosystem -- A continent for science -- Map -- Charts -- Studying
climate change -- Economics and the environment -- The Antarctic treaty
system -- Time line of events -- Concept web -- Quiz.
  ISBN 1-58340-356-6 (lib. bdg. : alk. paper)
  1. Antarctica--Juvenile literature. [1. Antarctica.] I. Title. II.
Series.
  G863.B63 2003
  919.8'9--dc21

                                    2002156591

                              Printed in Malaysia
                              2 4 6 8 9 7 5 3 1

EDITOR Nicole Bezic King **COPY EDITOR** Jennifer Nault
TEXT ADAPTATION Jonathan Bocknek **DESIGNER** Terry Paulhus
LAYOUT Terry Paulhus **PHOTO RESEARCHER** Nicole Bezic King
SERIES EDITOR Jennifer Nault **CREATIVE COMPANY EDITOR** Jill Weingartz

Contents

Introduction

Antarctica, one of Earth's continents, is the most inhospitable environment in the world. There are no farms, no forests, and no trees of any kind. The weather is colder, drier, and windier than anywhere on Earth. Thick sheets of ice cover 98 percent of the land. Bare rock makes up the remaining two percent. Antarctica boasts the world record for lowest temperature. In 1983, a temperature of −129 °F (−89.2 °C) was recorded at Vostok, a Russian research station on the continent. Why, then, does this desolate place attract such international interest and concern?

Antarctica has no **indigenous** human population. The only people who live there are researchers from different countries, and most of them live there only semi-permanently. Though many countries have laid claim to it, Antarctica belongs to no one. In a sense, the fifth-largest continent on Earth belongs to everyone.

Since Antarctic exploration began, seven nations have laid formal claims to portions of the continent and the waters and islands surrounding it: Argentina, Australia, Chile, France, New Zealand, Norway, and the United Kingdom. Many of these claims overlap. In the 1950s, at the height of the **Cold War**, the potential for conflict over territorial claims in Antarctica, particularly between the United States and the Soviet

Union, began to cause serious concern. The tension was defused by a diplomatic solution—the Antarctic **Treaty**. Signed in 1959, this treaty became effective in 1961. The seven claimant nations, as well as Belgium, Japan, South Africa, Russia (then known as the Soviet Union), and the U.S., agreed to treat Antarctica as a zone to be used purely for scientific research and cooperation. Military use of the continent was banned, and territorial claims have been put on hold indefinitely.

The Antarctic Treaty, along with several agreements that later accompanied it, represents a major step forward in protecting

Earth's "last wilderness." The most recent of these, the **Protocol** on Environmental Protection to the Antarctic Treaty (also known as the Environmental Protocol to the Antarctic Treaty, or the Madrid Protocol) was signed in 1991.

Antarctica offers a window on the past, present, and future of our planet.

Signing of the protocol was a great victory for those concerned with protecting the environment and through it, the planet. By banning commercial mining activities and introducing strict environmental regulations, the protocol has strengthened Antarctica's status as a natural reserve for peace and science. Even so, there are weaknesses in the treaty system. All diplomatic decisions are based on **consensus**. Thus, a single country can veto any proposal that it finds unacceptable. In addition, the treaty system lacks a permanent monitoring body. Instead, decisions are made at annual meetings held in different locations throughout the world.

As with any international treaty, successful implementation depends on the willingness of governments to enforce regulations over their own nationals. Without an

Antarctica, the planet's last wilderness, is a fragile environment at risk due to human activity.

independent monitoring body, effective enforcement is difficult. The situation is further complicated by the remoteness and climate of Antarctica, and the lack of a large and permanent population to "blow the whistle" on those who ignore or defy treaty agreements.

There are other difficulties as well. Some countries with an established presence in Antarctica still have not signed the Environmental Protocol. Overfishing in Antarctic waters, which has plagued the region for nearly 200 years, remains a problem. Baited fishing nets are killing seabirds by the thousands. Each Antarctic spring, a "hole" opens in the **ozone** layer over the South Pole. As a result, temperatures are increasing. This may be causing ice shelves to crumble, and could be an indication of global warming. Antarctic sea currents, which affect sea currents throughout the world, also appear to be changing. Tourism is increasing, and with it the potential for local environmental damage.

The Antarctic **ecosystem** is very fragile. Until the 1800s, the continent knew nothing of humans, or their often-punishing impact on the environment. As the world's last unspoiled wilderness, Antarctica offers a unique window on the past, present, and future of our planet. The health of the "white continent" both affects and serves as a barometer for the health of the rest of the planet.

Heroes of the Ice Continent

The first recorded voyage south of the Antarctic Circle was made by Captain James Cook in 1772–1775, while on his second expedition around the world. The Antarctic continent itself remained a mystery for more than 40 years, until it was eventually discovered by rival British and Russian expeditions between 1819 and 1821. Both Britain and Russia claimed first discovery. The dispute was not resolved until 1955, when an International Court of Justice ruled that the British expedition, led by Edward Bransfield, had been the first to discover Antarctica, on January 30, 1820.

Seal-hunting and whaling inspired most 19th-century voyages to Antarctic waters. In 1901, as interest in the science of geography grew, the International Geographic Congress proclaimed the "Year of the Antarctic." Over the next decade, various expeditions explored the Antarctic region, with the British being the first to formally claim territory in 1908. Whaling became a serious commercial activity in the region at this time. Within three decades, most of Antarctica was claimed by the British Empire and Norway, the two main whale-hunting nations. Argentina and Chile later made overlapping claims to part of "British Antarctica."

The first person to reach the South Pole was Norwegian explorer Roald Amundsen. He and his companions realized their goal on December 15, 1911. Four weeks later, a poorly prepared British expedition, led by Robert Falcon Scott, arrived at the South Pole only to find that the Norwegians had been there first. While Amundsen and his crew went on to live in Antarctica for one year, gathering scientific information and exploring new territory,

Captain James Cook's travels took him to the Pacific, Arctic, and Southern Oceans.

Scott and his three companions all perished on the way back. Like Amundsen, Scott also contributed valuable information to our understanding of Antarctica. His diaries and other documents were found and later published. The U.S. research station at the South Pole is named the Amundsen-Scott South Pole Station in honor of these two brave explorers.

By the 1920s, airplanes had become an established means of transportation. American Admiral Richard Byrd carried out the first flight over the South Pole in 1929. The use of airplanes transformed Antarctic exploration, making even the remotest and most inhospitable areas accessible.

Robert Falcon Scott (back row, middle) had already been to Antarctica once before his ill-fated race to the South Pole.

WHY WHALES?

Though whales had been hunted as food for centuries, it was not until the 1700s that whaling became a large-scale industry. Improved ships and hunting techniques made whaling easier. Whale by-products became more readily available as a result. Used to make corsets, soaps, and perfumes, whales were especially valued for their oil. Whale oil burns brightly and efficiently, and does not have much of an odor compared with the other animal fats and oils that were used to provide light and fuel for cooking. It is also an excellent **lubricating** oil, being sold for this purpose in the U.S. until the late 1970s. By the mid-1850s, kerosene lamps replaced whale-oil lamps, and the fledgling petroleum industry was in the process of gearing up. Without fossil fuels as alternative energy resources, and in the absence of a substitute for whale oil, most whale species today would likely be extinct.

It also meant that exploration and study could be carried out in relative comfort.

The modern age of international exploration of Antarctica began in the 1950s, led largely by scientists rather than explorers. American scientists developed a variety of research projects in Antarctica, as did scientists from the United Kingdom, the former Soviet Union, and other countries.

These scientists were the new pioneers, and their efforts continue today under the umbrella of the Scientific Committee on Antarctic Research (SCAR).

Due to a phenomenon called season reversal, while it is summer in Antarctica, it is winter in the northern hemisphere. Antarctic summer, therefore, happens at the same time as winter in North America.

One of the more recent "first-crossings" of the continent was achieved during the Antarctic summer of 1989/1990 by Reinhold Messner and Arved Fuchs. The two men successfully crossed Antarctica on foot. During that same summer, an international expedition under French leadership crossed Antarctica from west to east for

SHACKLETON'S MISSIONS

One of the most spectacular events in the history of Antarctic exploration occurred between 1914 and 1916. British adventurer Ernest Shackleton, already a veteran of two Antarctic expeditions, set out with 27 men on a quest to be the first to cross Antarctica on foot. He planned on crossing the continent from the Weddell Sea to the Ross Sea via the South Pole. In January 1915, within one day of reaching land, Shackleton's ship, the *Endurance*, became trapped in pack ice. Ten months later, the ship was finally crushed by the surrounding ice, and the crew spent a further five months camped on the ice while Shackleton planned his next move. Abandoning his original goal, Shackleton's new aim was simple—to get all of his men out alive. He led an 800-mile (1,287 km) voyage in a lifeboat to reach South Georgia, an island far off the coast of Antarctica. Pushing further

over mountains, Shackleton reached a whaling station on the island, and was able to organize a successful mission to rescue his crew.

Upon returning home from Antarctica, Ernest Shackleton recorded his experiences in his second book, called *South*, published in 1919 (his first book, *The Heart of Antarctica*, was published in 1909). He gave lectures about his earlier expeditions, including one in which he had accompanied Robert Falcon Scott. In 1921, Shackleton organized one last trip to the Antarctic. This time his goal was to sail around the continent in search of unknown islands, charting new territory. At Grytviken, South Georgia, on January 5, 1922, Shackleton suffered a massive heart attack aboard his ship. His wife, Emily, insisted he be buried on the island of South Georgia, in the Antarctic.

the first time, using dogsleds. The intent underlying both expeditions was to bring the importance and vulnerability of Antarctica to world attention at a time when the Antarctic Treaty System appeared to be under threat. It was at this time that various nations were considering the continent for its mining potential. Further assistance was provided by celebrated **oceanographer** Jacques Cousteau. In 1990, Cousteau launched a special trip to the Antarctic. Aboard his ship were six children, each representing one of the other six continents. The Lilliput Expedition, as it was called, together with a successful petition campaign, helped pave the way for the Environmental Protocol to the Antarctic Treaty.

Ernest Shackleton's hut at Cape Royd remains as he left it nearly 100 years ago. Dry, cold weather and efforts to protect such sites mean that the huts and equipment of early Antarctic explorers have been well preserved.

This old, rusting whaling ship at Grytviken, South Georgia, serves as a reminder of Antarctica's once-flourishing whaling industry.

KEY CONCEPTS

Antarctic Circle The Antarctic Circle is the name given to the 66°30′ S parallel of latitude. South of this latitude, the sun never rises on the "summer" solstice (around June 21), and it never sets on the "winter" solstice (around December 21). Periods of continuous day or night increase the closer one gets to the South Pole, from one day at the Antarctic Circle to six months at the Pole.

Scientific Committee on Antarctic Research (SCAR) SCAR was formed in 1958 to continue the scientific cooperation established during the International Geophysical Year (IGY) of 1957/1958. This committee is not formally recognized as being part of the Antarctic Treaty System (ATS). Even so, SCAR is the principal provider of independent technical advice to meetings of the Consultative Parties. In effect, it acts as the scientific coordinating body for the treaty.

SCAR also works with the International Council of Scientific Unions to coordinate polar-related projects that have global significance. SCAR holds the world's largest collection of aerial photographs of Antarctica.

Season reversal As Earth's axis tilts toward the sun, the climate becomes warmer. Similarly, as Earth's axis tilts away from the sun, the climate cools. As a result, the seasons are reversed in the Southern Hemisphere. So, while it is winter in the Northern Hemisphere, it is summer in the Southern Hemisphere.

Born: September 29, 1955, in Mendota Heights, Minnesota
Legacy: First known woman to trek to the North and South Poles; one of two women to be the first to trek across Antarctica

For more information on Ann Bancroft head to **www.ann bancroftfoundation.org/** and **www.yourexpedition.com/** to share her experiences and learn about the achievement of dreams.

People in Focus

On November 13, 2000, Ann Bancroft, along with Norwegian explorer Liv Arnesen, set out on a 1,717-mile (2,763 km) journey to wind sail and ski across the Antarctic continent. After 94 days they completed their trek, becoming the first women to cross the continent "on foot." Equally remarkable was their dream: to bring the children of the world along with them, via the Internet.

With a Bachelor of Science degree in physical education, Bancroft has taught physical and special education. She is also among the world's most renowned polar explorers, and is an accomplished motivational public speaker. Through her polar expeditions and the Ann Bancroft Foundation, she seeks to inspire women, young and old alike, to share and pursue their dreams.

Bancroft is also the first woman to cross both the North and South Poles. In 1986, she became the first known woman to travel by dogsled to the North Pole from Canada's Northwest Territories (now divided into the Northwest Territories and Nunavut). In 1993, she led a 67-day, 660-mile (1,060 km) skiing expedition to the South Pole.

Bancroft's Antarctic adventure with Liv Arnesen has already inspired students from all over the world. Through a special Web site, www.yourexpedition.com, people across the globe can relive this remarkable accomplishment. In December 2001, Bancroft and Arnesen returned to Antarctica to kayak through the Antarctic Peninsula. Their most recent adventure took them across North America's Great Lakes in May and June of 2002.

Wherever she goes, Bancroft continues to share her dreams and knowledge, and inspires others to do the same.

Land of Extremes

The Antarctic region stretches north of the Antarctic Circle to include the area bounded by the Antarctic Convergence. This is a band of sea between about 50 and 60 °S in which the waters of the southern and northern oceans mix. The waters surrounding the continent are often collectively referred to as the Southern or Antarctic Ocean.

The continent itself has a total area larger than the U.S. and Mexico combined— about 7,456,454 square miles (12 million sq km), with an additional 994,194 square miles (1.6 million sq km) in the form of ice shelves. In winter, freezing of the seas can extend the continent to twice its summer size. Antarctica is commonly divided into two regions, West Antarctica and East Antarctica. West Antarctica is a group of mountainous islands bonded together and covered by ice. East Antarctica is three times as large as its western counterpart. It consists mainly of a great ice-covered plateau.

Antarctica has a total area larger than the U.S. and Mexico combined.

The two regions are divided by the Transantarctic Mountains. This impressive range runs across the continent for about 1,864 miles (3,000 km). With an average height of 8,200 feet (2,500 m), Antarctica is three times as high as the other continents. Its **continental shelves** are also four to seven times deeper.

The continent is almost circular in shape. A narrow peninsula about 800 miles (1,287 km) long extends toward Tierra del Fuego in South America. The northern portion of the peninsula is known as Graham Land. The southern portion is called Palmer Land. The peninsula is often referred to simply as the Antarctic Peninsula.

Almost 620 miles (1,000 km) away from Antarctica, is South America, the nearest continent. Australia is about 2,300 miles (3,700 km) away, and South Africa is about 2,600 miles (4,200 km) from the Antarctic landmass. A number of small volcanic islands in between

WOULD THE REAL SOUTH POLE PLEASE STAND UP!

There are three South Poles. One is the geographic South Pole, which is near the Amundsen-Scott South Pole Station in East Antarctica. It is the place where all the lines of longitude meet. Each year, the geographic South Pole must be re-marked. This is because the ice sheet moves about 1.1 inches (2.8 cm) every day. Another South Pole, located closer to the Amundsen-Scott South Pole Station, is ceremonial. It is marked with a red-and-white-striped post with a reflective sphere attached at the top. Flags from different countries surround it. Unlike the geographic South Pole, this one is not re-marked annually. It simply moves with the flowing ice. The third South Pole is the magnetic South Pole. This is the place that compass needles in the Northern Hemisphere point away from. More precisely, it is a point on Earth where the magnetic lines of force are oriented vertically upwards. Earth's magnetic poles move because its magnetic field moves. In 1909, the magnetic South Pole was located on the Antarctic landmass. Today, it is in the Antarctic Ocean, about 1,775 miles (2,856 km) away from Antarctica.

have been claimed over the years by different countries.

Only about two percent of Antarctica's total area is bare rock. Much of this is found at the shoreline. The rest of the landmass is covered in a layer of ice that is about 1.25 miles (2 km) thick on average. The volume of this ice is about 72 million cubic miles (30 million cu km). This represents close to 90 percent of all Earth's glacial ice. It also makes up about 70 percent of the world's freshwater. Despite this vast amount of water, yearly precipitation for most of the continent is less than two inches (50 mm). In effect, Antarctica is a desert.

Most of Antarctica's many mountains are hidden beneath a thick layer of ice.

Only about five percent of the coast is free of ice. Surrounding the coastline are massive ice shelves. These floating fringes of ice rise and fall with the tides. The largest, the Ross Ice Shelf, is about the size of France. Ice that breaks free of an ice shelf forms icebergs. Only about one-fifth of an iceberg is visible above water. Icebergs may take several years to melt as they float northward into warmer areas.

Antarctica is Earth's stormiest and windiest continent. Katabatic, or "downslope," winds rage at the coast, reaching speeds as high as 200 miles (320 km) per hour. Elsewhere on the continent, average wind speeds are more modest, averaging 12 miles (19 km) per hour. The combination of powerful winds with blowing or falling snow often produces blizzards. Extreme wind chill conditions are also common.

Antarctica's abundant ice may one day supply freshwater to places with limited resources. Towing icebergs—some the size of small countries—to arid regions is being seriously considered.

KEY CONCEPTS

Antarctic Convergence This band of sea encircles the Antarctic continent. It is also known as the Polar Front. This zone, found between 47 and 62 °S, is a place where the cold, dense waters of the polar region meet the warmer, saltier waters of the Atlantic, Pacific, and Indian Oceans. The position of this natural zone varies only slightly from year to year. Thus it serves as a convenient ecological boundary for Antarctica.

Blizzards Most people associate blizzards with heavy snowfall. In fact, a blizzard requires no snowfall at all. Blizzards involve strong winds of 35 miles per hour (56 km/h) or more, coupled with low visibility due to blowing or falling snow. Antarctic blizzards are usually caused by wind raising settled snow. They are frequent in the Antarctic, especially during the winter, and may last for weeks at a time.

Ice sheets and ice shelves The Antarctic continent is blanketed with large, thick masses of ice called ice sheets. Fast-moving

Though scenic, Antarctica presents many challenges for those who choose to visit, work, or live there.

rivers of ice flow through the ice sheets, drawing some ice along with them and carrying it out to the ocean. The result is ice shelves—floating expanses of ice that remain attached to the land. The East Antarctic ice sheet covers an area of 3,844,000 square miles (10,000,000 sq km)—about the size of Australia. The smaller West Antarctic ice sheet comprises an area one-fifth of that. Together, these ice sheets contain roughly 90 percent of Earth's ice.

Katabatic winds Complex patterns of air movement and temperature change create winds that blow down the mountains and coastal **escarpments** of Antarctica. Impelled further by gravity, these downward-flowing winds can surge toward the sea at ferocious speeds. They are called katabatic winds (katabatic means "to go down"). While not unique to Antarctica, they are one of its distinctive weather features.

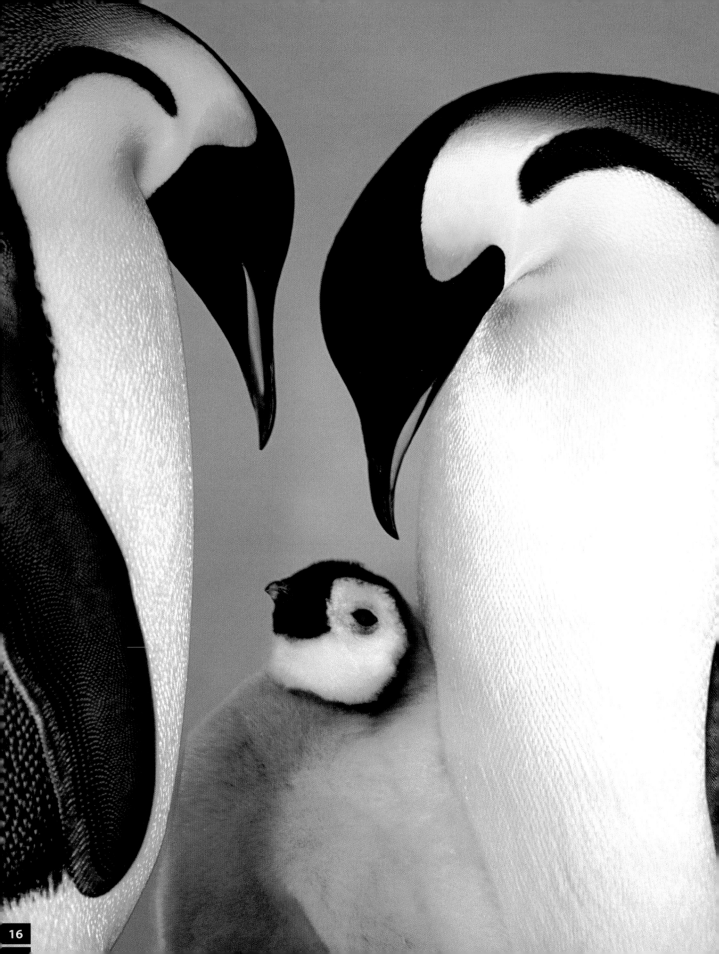

A Fragile Ecosystem

It is no surprise that the planet's highest, driest, coldest, windiest continent has little in the way of local **flora**. There are no trees, and only two species of flowering plants are known to exist on the continent. These are found on the Antarctic Peninsula. Algae crowd the surrounding seas, and some are adapted to survive on the snow-covered land surface. Patches of **lichen** cover many rocky outcrops. Mosses and liverworts make up the remaining vegetation. In recent years, vegetation on the Antarctic Peninsula appears to have been increasing. Some scientists consider this to be a sign of global warming, though other parts of Antarctica have shown little evidence of increased temperatures and plant life.

No mammals live on the Antarctic mainland. In fact, there are few animals of any kind. Local **fauna** are all **invertebrates**, the largest of which is a midge about 0.2 inches (5 mm) long. Mites and springtails, which are tiny wingless insects, are the most plentiful of these.

There are approximately 200,000 breeding pairs of emperor penguins in Antarctica. They live in 40 different colonies that range in size from a few hundred to 20,000 pairs.

Life in this harsh climate is precariously balanced. Such a delicate balance can be upset easily. Pollution and even noise disturbance can have a disastrous impact on local ecosystems.

> ### *Pollution can have a disastrous impact on local ecosystems.*

Even mild disturbances can have damaging effects. For example, birds startled by photographers may abandon their nests, leaving chicks exposed to the killing cold. Antarctica's meager vegetation is easily damaged by careless human contact.

In warmer climates, all organic waste, from paper to excrement, decomposes fairly quickly with the help of insects, worms, and **microbes**. In Antarctica, however, such organisms are scarce. Most waste simply freezes. Even iron does not rust easily in the dry air. Wood and fabric do not rot, leaving huts and equipment from the earliest expeditions in the same condition as they were a century ago. Fortunately, there are now strict regulations governing the management of waste in Antarctica. For example, the British Antarctic Survey (BAS), which runs a number of research stations in the region, requires that all but food waste and sewage be removed from Antarctica. Despite such regulations and practices, some negative impact due to human contact is unavoidable.

PENGUINS BY THE THOUSANDS

Many people think penguins live at both the North and South Poles. Penguins, however, are south-polar only. They are, perhaps, the animal most closely associated with Antarctica. Large colonies have populations running into many thousands. Of the 17 penguin species, only one—the emperor penguin—stays on Antarctica throughout the winter. A male emperor spends a large part of the winter standing on the polar ice with an egg lying on his feet. This incubation period lasts about two months. During this time, the male does not eat and drinks only snow while keeping the egg warm under a flap of abdominal skin. Males huddle with hundreds of others as they shuffle for position on the ice. Those on the outside, where it is coldest, gradually change position with those on the warmer inside.

KRILL IS THE KEY

Krill are shrimp-like animals, about 2.5 inches (6 cm) in size. They are at the heart of all Antarctic **food webs**. A single group may extend for great distances, with a mass of several million tons. Krill are food for baleen whales. In fact, their name is derived from the Norwegian word for "whale food." They are also the main source of nutrition for many species of fish, seabirds, seal, and squid. About 110,230 tons (100,000 t) of krill are legally caught each year.

A better understanding of krill and their ecological role is needed. Commercial demand may be increasing, and recent evidence suggests that stocks may be declining, perhaps due to global warming. Current fishing practices are also thought to be adversely affecting krill stocks and, in turn, their predators. The problem seems to lie in when and where krill is being harvested, rather than the numbers being harvested. For example, fishers may be forcing young penguins to go further afield for their food, exposing them to increased danger from their predators.

In contrast to the mainland, life at the coastal rim is wonderfully diverse. Some 100 million penguins live in Antarctica. The region is also home to millions of other birds and huge colonies of seals. The nutrient-rich seas heave with krill and their predators, such as fish, squid, and whales. Regulations covering the commercial harvesting of this abundance are set out in the Convention on the Conservation of Antarctic Marine Living Resources (CCAMLR).

Regulations are vital to the natural and commercial health of Antarctic marine life. Early explorers were quick to exploit the region's abundance. For example, the voyages of Captain James Weddell and other early explorers led what were essentially sealing expeditions. Fur seals and elephant seals were killed in huge numbers, and by 1822, fur seals were already becoming scarce. By the end of the century, the elephant seal was also rare. A **convention** for the protection of Antarctic seals was finally established in 1972. Populations of fur and elephant seals have begun to recover as a result.

Whaling began in earnest in the Antarctic in 1904, and soon became big business. More than 1,000,000 Antarctic whales were killed in the 20th century. In the 1930/1931 season alone, about 30,000 blue whales were killed. Large numbers of humpback and sperm whales also perished. The blue whale, the largest animal on Earth, has been an endangered species ever since.

While populations of fur seals have recovered since hunting was banned, the same cannot be said of the whale population. Many species remain rare, even though they have been protected for two decades or more. The decline in whale populations has changed the ecological balance in Antarctica, the effects of which are not yet fully understood.

Even the beloved penguin has not escaped commercial exploitation. On Macquarie Island, young penguins coming ashore to molt used to be herded into pens. They were then clubbed and thrown into digesters, in which they were boiled to extract the oil from their fat. The Macquarie Island

Unafraid of humans, Antarctic wildlife provides amusement—and excellent photo opportunities—for visitors to Antarctica.

factory alone killed about 150,000 penguins per year before public opinion eventually forced its closure. The island became a wildlife sanctuary in 1933.

Despite such atrocities, Antarctic animals generally remain unafraid of humans. People are able to get closer to wildlife here than anywhere else on Earth. Such close encounters are an important part of Antarctica's tourist appeal.

LIFE IN THE FRIGID WATER

Most fish could not survive in Antarctic waters. The water is colder than the freezing point of their blood. The fish that inhabit Antarctic waters are well-adapted to this unique environment. Their blood contains proteins that allow it to remain in a liquid state. These "antifreeze" proteins bond to ice crystals in their bodies, preventing more crystals from accumulating. This saves cells and tissue from damage. Scientists are studying these proteins for possible medical and commercial applications.

Southern elephant seals are among the six species of seal found in the Antarctic. Once under threat, their numbers have now stabilized.

KEY CONCEPTS

Adaptations Adaptations are physical features and behaviors that make an organism well-suited for a particular way of life or environment. For example, the "antifreeze" proteins in the blood of Antarctic fish are an adaptation that lets them survive and thrive in the Southern Ocean. Penguins and seals are common inhabitants of the Antarctic region, but they lack these blood proteins. Instead, they have a different adaptation that protects their blood from freezing: insulation. Their blubber is extremely effective at maintaining the temperature of their blood. The coloration of some Antarctic birds, notably petrels, is another adaptation to their way of life. For example, the white plumage of snow petrels allows them to blend into the whiteness of the icebergs and pack ice they live near. Their eggs are also white—a further protection against predators.

All organisms are adapted to their environment, not just animals. For example, the plants that live in the Antarctic have adaptations such as densely packed stems and shoots that enable them to conserve water. Many Antarctic plants contain antifreeze-like compounds that allow them to survive repeated freezing and thawing. Some plants also contain molecules that act as a sunscreen. These molecules protect them from the intensity of the sun's ultraviolet radiation.

Convention on the Conservation of Antarctic Marine Living Resources (CCAMLR) Adopted in 1980 but in force since 1982, this convention is part of the Antarctic Treaty System. Its mandate is to protect marine life south of the Antarctic Convergence. The permanent CCAMLR secretariat is based in North Hobart, Tasmania.

CCAMLR uses an ecological border (the Antarctic Convergence) rather than latitude to mark its territory of influence. Annual meetings are held to determine, on the basis of scientific advice, how much of each species of crab, fish, krill, and squid may be caught in defined areas of the Southern Ocean. In setting quotas and imposing bans, the effect on other animals in the food web is considered. Seals are subject to a separate convention, while management of whales is handled by the International Whaling Commission (IWC).

Marine Biologist

Duties: Studies marine life forms and their relationships with each other and their environment
Education: Bachelor of Science degree, and a Master of Science degree. Sometimes a Ph.D. may even be required.
Interests: Marine life, working outdoors, environmental issues, and the sea

For further information on a career in marine biology, head to **www.siograddept.ucsd.edu/ Web/To_Be_A_Marine_Biologist. html** and **www.marinecareers.net**

Careers in Focus

Marine biologists study plants and animals that live in the sea and connected bodies of water. In addition to studying their anatomy, development, origins, and functions, they also examine the relationships among and between marine life forms and their environment. Marine biologists seek to better understand the impact of pollution and other natural and human factors.

Marine biologists must generally be in good physical shape. Although some of their work is conducted indoors in laboratories, a great deal also takes place outdoors, where marine life can be observed in its natural environment. A love of the sea is essential, as extended periods spent at sea or at shore-based field stations are often required.

Marine biologists can also expect to scuba dive and work on commercial fishing vessels. In preparation, they should enjoy and be good at swimming and boating.

Like any scientist, marine biologists must have excellent analytical, numerical, and statistical skills, and be accurate and precise in all their work. Office work, including preparing long reports on research findings, is also an important part of the job. Marine biologists may be required to design and carry out experiments, advise on the introduction and control of species, and make recommendations to the appropriate bodies based on their findings. They may even be required to provide advice to politicians, business managers, and the general public. Unfortunately for some, marine biology is not only about swimming with penguins and dolphins!

A Continent for Science

With the exception of sealing and whaling expeditions, most Antarctic expeditions have been aimed at improving scientific knowledge. Antarctica's unspoiled environment makes it an ideal laboratory for a wide range of scientific areas, including biology, astronomy, geology, and many other disciplines. Cooperation and research in the Antarctic has greatly increased our understanding of problems such as global warming and the hole in the ozone layer. Research sharing has also enhanced our knowledge of marine biology, oceanography, and many other science branches.

The number of Antarctic research stations multiplied in the 1980s, when scientific involvement was necessary in order for Antarctic Treaty nations to be able to vote on

issues concerning the region. As of 2002, there were 44 winter stations. More open during the summer months. Though nearly all are run by treaty nations, there is nothing to stop non-member nations from setting up their own research stations.

Stations vary greatly in size. Many are little more than a hut and a few instruments. Others have become small polar villages. For example, the Argentinean station at Esperanza has a supermarket, post office, and church. It provides 287,000 square yards (240,000 sq m) of space to accommodate personnel and their families.

Antarctica's unspoiled environment makes it an ideal laboratory for a wide range of scientific areas.

The National Science Foundation (NSF) runs the American stations. Work began in 1999 on a new upgrade to the

Scientists must observe guidelines set out by the Antarctic Treaty System when conducting their research.

Amundsen-Scott South Pole station, where Americans have been living since 1956. Unlike the original base, long since buried under snowdrifts, the third and newest one will be able to be jacked up when necessary to keep it above the drifts. Construction is scheduled to finish in 2006.

The main U.S. base—and the largest research station in Antarctica—is at McMurdo, on the southern end of Ross Island. Established in 1956, the settlement houses 250 people over the winter. Another 850 people arrive in the summer months. With more than 100 buildings and a busy airport nearby, McMurdo is the focal point for all American science activity in the Antarctic.

AN ICY LOOK INTO THE UNIVERSE

Imagine a telescope so technologically advanced that it allows scientists to peer into the past and learn more about the formation of the universe. Scientists from the U.S. and several other countries are building just such a device in Antarctica. The device, a "telescope" known as Ice Cube, will use neutrino detectors to analyze 0.25 cubic miles (1 cu km) of ice. Lying 1.5 miles (2.4 km) below the Antarctic surface, Ice Cube will be able to detect the presence of high-energy neutrinos and trace their history. Using Ice Cube, scientists will be able to measure and chart the path of neutrinos as they travel from space through Earth. As the smallest particles of matter, neutrinos are virtually massless particles that are able to pass from one object to another without interference. Since neutrinos can only be seen in rare conditions, Antarctica is the ideal location for Ice Cube. The deep, dark, transparent, and expansive Antarctic ice is a perfect place to capture and observe neutrinos. This research will help scientists learn more about distant astronomical bodies such as black holes and exploding stars.

Although these research stations belong to a variety of nations, there is a high degree of cooperation among scientists from different countries. For example, the United States has worked with Britain on geology and seal biology, while France and Russia have worked together on a deep-ice drilling program.

Rocks and sea sediments help scientists study Earth's climatic past going back over millions of years. Ice cores can give a detailed picture of Earth's climate in the more recent past. Long, hollow pipes are drilled deep into the ice, and cores of ice are removed. Each core shows distinct layers, with each layer representing a year or season of accumulation.

One ice core from the Russian station at Vostok was more than 6,562 feet (2,000 m) in length. It was able to provide climate information going back over the past 160,000 years. Ice cores contain valuable information about the past composition of the atmosphere and can show past pollution levels. For example, scientists can track changes in the build-up of carbon dioxide over time. Such information helps researchers gain a better understanding of the greenhouse effect and global warming.

Antarctica is rich in fossils. Fossilized plants show that Antarctica's climate was once very different from today. In fact, the presence of beech tree and other plant fossils are compelling evidence that the continent was once located far from its present place. According to the Gondwanaland theory, Antarctica was positioned north of the equator about 240 million years ago.

Fossil discoveries help scientists learn about Earth's history, as well as the history

WHAT TO WEAR?

Living and working in the Antarctic requires special clothing considerations. The United States Antarctic Program (USAP) issues special gear to its personnel that is suitable for extreme cold weather (ECW). Some of these items include:

- 1 polar fleece balaclava (a type of ski mask)

- 1 pair of "bunny boots" (a kind of insulated rubber boot)

- 6 pairs of woolen tube socks

- 1 pair each of various kinds of mittens

- 1 pair of polar fleece pants

- 1 red parka

- 1 polar fleece jacket

- 1 pair each of various thermal undershirts and underwear

of its life forms. In the same way, thousands of meteorites found in Antarctica have furthered scientific research. Scientists use these deposits from outer space to learn about our solar system—and beyond.

Current research in biology focuses on krill and their vital role in Antarctic food webs. Other areas of scientific interest include the study of ocean currents and Earth's magnetic field. Not surprisingly, ice and the ozone hole are key points of interest as well.

One benefit of working in extreme conditions is the valuable psychological and medical research that can result. Researchers live in cramped quarters and have limited contact with the outside world. Antarctic winters are long and dark. The sun does not shine for months at a time. People in Antarctica have been, and sometimes still are, used for experiments in human behavior and **physiology**.

Since ice cores can only be retrieved in short sections, it takes months and even years to retrieve cores of significant length.

Leaf fossils found in Antarctica indicate that the continent was once heavily forested. Dinosaur and other animal fossils have also been found in the region.

KEY CONCEPTS

Global warming The average temperature on Earth is increasing. Although this may be due in part to natural variation, many scientists believe the increase in temperature is largely a result of industrial processes and can ultimately lead to changes in climate. When the climate changes, so do patterns of rainfall and sea levels. Climate change can affect plants and animals in various ways.

Gondwanaland Why are there fossils from temperate forests hidden beneath the Antarctic ice? The theory of **plate tectonics**, and one of its mechanisms, continental drift, is one answer. The Gondwanaland theory states that about 240 million years ago, Antarctica was part of a large landmass—a supercontinent. This supercontinent was comprised of Africa, India, South America, and Australia. About 150 million years ago, this landmass, referred to as Gondwanaland, began to split up. These parts eventually drifted to their current locations. Evidence from a variety of scientific fields supports this theory.

Greenhouse effect Energy radiated by the sun travels to Earth and warms the surface. Some of this energy becomes trapped in the atmosphere by gases such as carbon dioxide. As a result, the lower portion of Earth's atmosphere experiences a rise in temperature. Most scientists acknowledge the greenhouse effect, but there is much debate about its causes and effects.

Scientific cooperation Antarctic researchers from different stations often work together on joint projects. Such collaboration is a model for the international community. It is also a central feature of scientific work in general. Either directly or through letters or electronic mail, scientists have always communicated with one another. This is the way much of our scientific understanding has developed.

Duties: Studies glaciers and other ice formations in order to assess their effects on the landscape and climate

Education: Bachelor of Science degree in geosciences

Interests: Working outdoors, prehistory, the environment, and technology

For further information on glaciology, navigate to **www.geog.le.ac.uk/ cti/glac.html**, or consult **www.schoolsinwashin gton.com/usa/careerprofiles_ details.cfm?CarID=394**

Careers in Focus

People have been collecting climate data for a relatively short period of human history. With few exceptions, reliable records go back only several hundred years. Fortunately, ice stores a record of Earth's history that extends several hundred thousand years into the past. The story of global warming is written in ice.

Glacial ice has unique properties. Neither fully liquid nor fully solid, glaciers move. The snowflakes that eventually form ice contain substances and materials that were in the air when the snow first fell to Earth. These include oxygen, carbon dioxide, soot, ashes, and various other chemicals and particles.

Glaciologists can make inferences about climate conditions of the past and present by studying these substances. One technique they use involves taking ice cores. Using these samples, glaciologists have shown that Earth's atmosphere has changed over time. For example, the amount of carbon dioxide has increased and decreased several times over the past several hundred thousand years, though the accumulation of greenhouse gases has never been as high as today. Periods of increase in greenhouse gases seem to occur at the same time as periods of significant climate change. Glaciologists examine these relationships to come up with reasonable explanations for these events.

In the Antarctic, glaciologists have almost an entire continent to study. They try to answer questions such as: Why are some of the ice shelves disintegrating so quickly? What is likely to happen to different areas of the continent over the next hundred or thousand years? How, if at all, are humans contributing to some of the processes being observed in Antarctica?

Mapping Antarctica

Figure 1: Antarctica

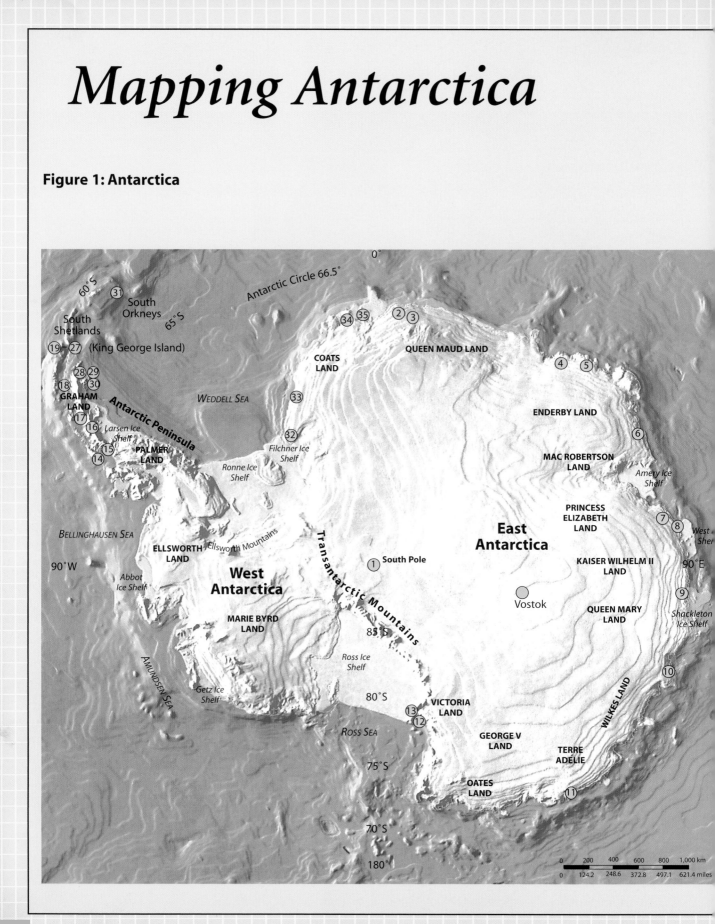

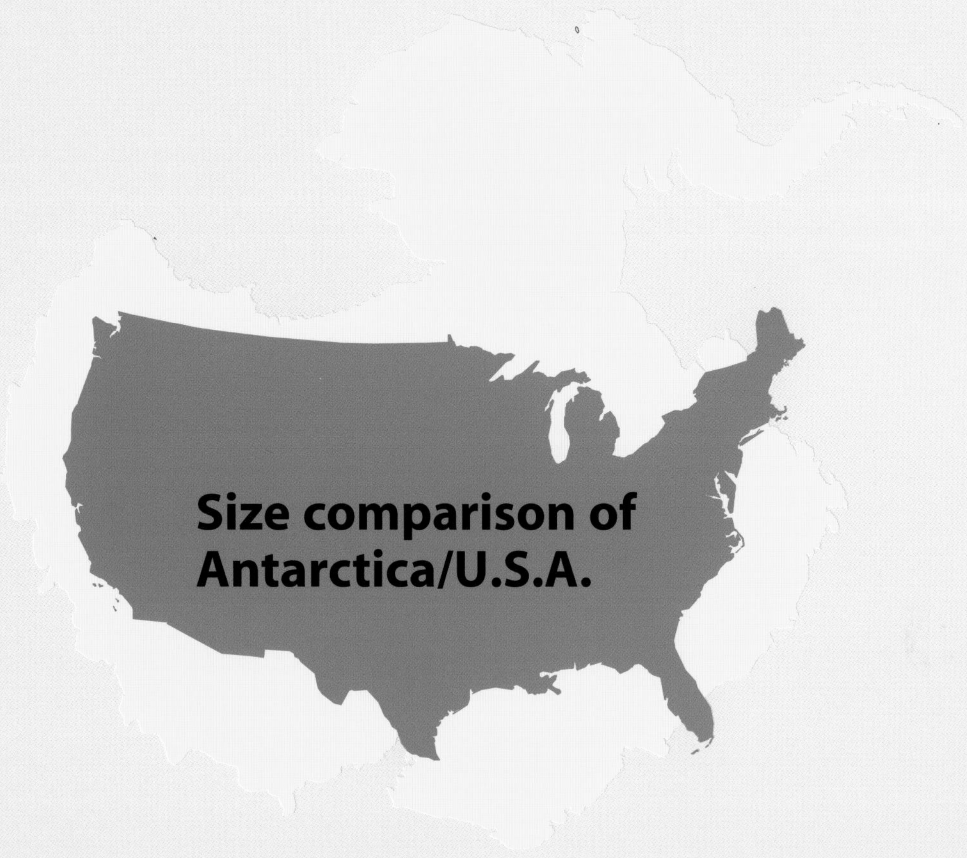

Size comparison of Antarctica/U.S.A.

**Research Stations
(operating in winter 2002)**

1   Amundsen-Scott (U.S.A.)
2   Maitri (India)
3   Novolazarevskaya (Russia)
4   Syowa (Japan)
5   Molodezhnaya (Russia)
6   Mawson (Australia)
7   Zhongshan (China)
8   Davis (Australia)
9   Mirny (Russia)
10 Casey (Australia)
11 Dumont d'Urville (France)
12 McMurdo (U.S.A.)
13 Scott Base (New Zealand)
14 Rothera (UK)
15 San Martin (Argentina)
16 Vernadsky (Ukraine)
17 Palmer (U.S.A.)
18 Capitan Arturo Prat (Chile)
19 Great Wall (China)
20 Bellinghausen (Russia)
21 Artigas (Uruguay)
22 King Sejong (South Korea)
23 Jubany (Argentina)
24 Arctowski (Poland)
25 Comandante Ferraz (Brazil)
26 Presidente Eduardo
      Frei (Chile)
27 Escudero (Chile)
28 General Bernardo
      O'Higgins (Chile)
29 Esperanza (Argentina)
30 Marambio (Argentina)
31 Orcadas (Argentina)
32 Belgrano II (Argentina)
33 Halley (UK)
34 Neumayer (Germany)
35 SANAE IV (South Africa)

North of 60°

Macquarie Island (Australia)
Alfred Faure, Iles Crozet (France)
Martin de Viviès, Ile
Amsterdam (France)
Port aux Français, Iles
Kerguelen (France)
Gough Island (South Africa)
Marion Island (South Africa)
Bird Island (UK)
King Edward Point, South
Georgia (UK)

Understanding Antarctica

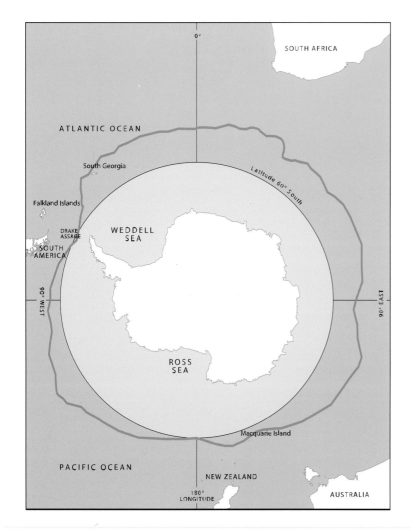

Figure 2: The Antarctic Region

☐ Area covered by the Antarctic Treaty

▬ Antarctic Convergence: Limit of area covered by the Convention on the Conservation of Antarctic Marine Living Resources (CCAMLR).

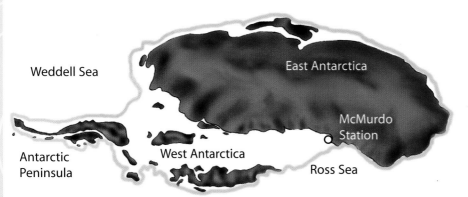

Figure 3: Antarctica Under the Ice

Seismic soundings and gravity measurements indicate that beneath the ice, Antarctica is much smaller than it appears.

Figure 4: The Gondwanaland "Puzzle"

The "puzzle" below shows Antarctica's geological connection with other mineral-rich continents.

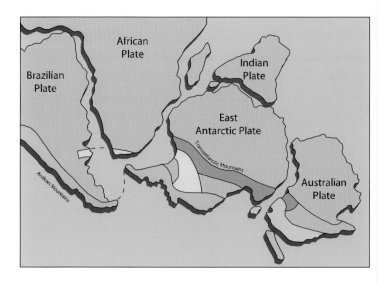

Figure 5: Territorial Claims

Under the Antarctic Treaty, all territorial claims have effectively been sidelined. Prior to 1959, seven countries had laid claim to parts of Antarctica, with Britain (in 1908) the first to register its interest. The U.S. and Russia have never made claims of their own, nor have they ever recognized other claims.

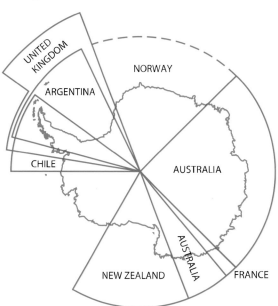

Figure 6: Sea Ice Extent

During the Antarctic winter, frozen seas increase the size of the continent to nearly twice its summer size.

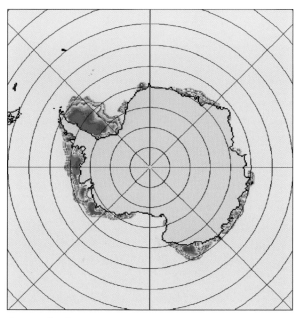

Antarctica in summer

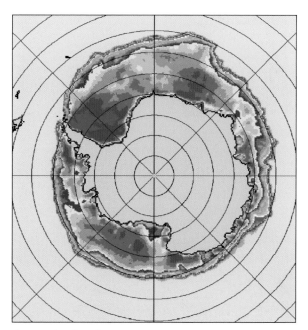

Antarctica in winter

Studying Climate Change

On the eastern side of the Antarctic Peninsula lies the Larsen Ice Shelf. Scientists estimate that it has existed for at least the past 400 years, and possibly as long as 12,000 years. On January 31, 2002, a portion of the ice shelf, called Larsen B, began to disintegrate. During the next 35 days, the shelf lost 1,255 square miles (3,250 sq km) of its area. From 1998 to the time of its spectacular collapse in early 2002, the area of the ice shelf had diminished by 40 percent.

Scientists with the British Antarctic Survey (BAS) had been monitoring the ice shelf throughout the 1990s. The dramatic collapse was expected. As one scientist put it, "In 1998, BAS predicted the demise of more ice shelves around the

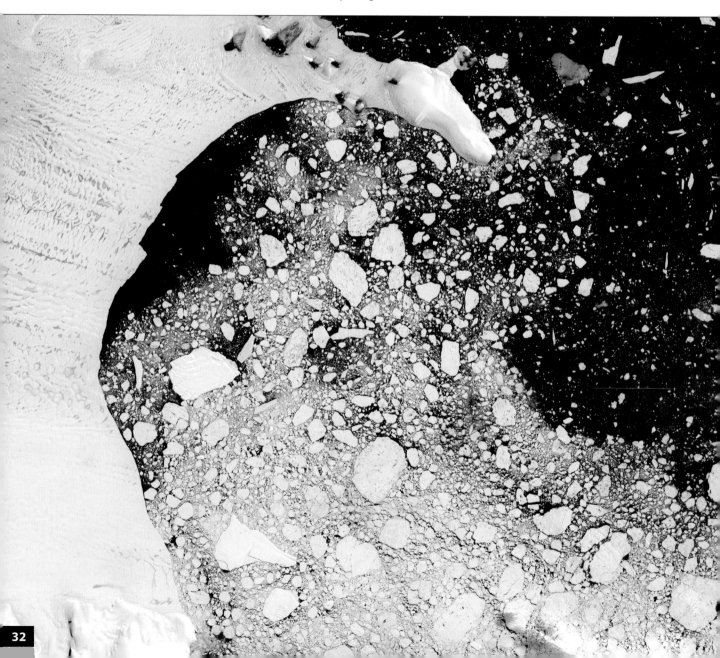

Antarctic Peninsula. Since then, warming on the peninsula has continued, and we watched as, piece-by-piece, Larsen B has retreated. We knew what was left would collapse eventually, but the speed of it is staggering." This particular scientist found it hard to believe that so much ice—equal to the size of Luxembourg, a small European country—had disintegrated in less than a month.

Larsen B is not the first ice shelf known to disappear from the continent's fringe. The Prince Gustav ice shelf near McMurdo is now gone. The Wordie ice shelf on the western side of the Peninsula has suffered a similar fate. By 1995, the northern tip of the Larsen Ice Shelf had already given way. Are these dramatic events evidence of global warming, or are they the result of natural fluctuations in global temperature?

Climate change is one of the most important areas of Antarctic research. The stability of the Antarctic ice sheets is especially important. Some research suggests that the total volume of the ice sheets has increased and decreased over the years. These changes have been both gradual, taking place over millions of years, as well

as sudden, occurring over only a few decades.

Other research suggests that the ice sheets overall have decreased in size over the last 2.5 million years. Global sea levels may have increased by 130 feet (40 m) as a result. If

---

By 1997, the ozone hole was more than twice the size of Europe.

---

this is true, the big question is whether this could happen again. If so, how long would it take? Equally important, is human activity accelerating the process?

In 1985, scientists had collected enough data to make a dire statement: Earth's protective ozone layer was being depleted, allowing more of the sun's rays through. The effects were most pronounced over Antarctica. The ozone hole that forms each spring is actually an area of greatly reduced ozone concentration. The size of this area of depletion increased dramatically between 1990

and 1997. By 1997, the ozone hole was more than twice the size of Europe. Since then, each year has brought new record or near-record increases in size.

Scientists continue to investigate the links between ozone depletion and global warming. One such link involves **chlorofluorocarbons** (CFCs). These compounds contribute to the greenhouse effect, and so are related to trends in global temperature increases.

International efforts to protect the ozone layer have been in place since the late 1980s. Adherence to agreements for reducing the use of ozone-depleting chemicals is expected to assist the rebuilding of the ozone layer. This is expected to start within the next decade. Even so, some of the chemicals used to replace CFCs have inspired a new threat. Hydrofluorocarbons (HFCs) are supposed to be "ozone-friendly," but they are also implicated in global warming. The reduction of HFCs is part of the Kyoto Protocol of 1997.

In February 2000, the Larsen B ice shelf was already splintering. When it finally collapsed in 2002, the area of ice lost from the shelf was larger than Rhode Island.

MEASURING OZONE

The amount of ozone in the atmosphere is measured in Dobson units (DU). A typical, healthy Dobson reading would be about 300 DU. In 1993, scientists recorded the lowest-measured amount of ozone yet over Antarctica—88 DU. The next year, the recorded value had increased to 98 DU, and in 2001 the Dobson reading again increased, to 100 DU. Despite slightly improved DU readings, the size of the ozone hole remains a cause for concern—as of 2001, it was slightly larger than the area of North America.

It is estimated that global temperatures have risen by 0.8 to 1.0 °F (0.45–0.6 °C) over the last century. The last decade of the 20th century was the hottest on record. Not surprisingly, global ice melting was recorded in more places and at greater rates during this same decade. Meanwhile, the mean global sea level has risen six to eight inches (10–20 cm) over the last 100 years. This may seem like a small amount. It is, however, greater than the rate of increase over the past several thousand years.

Since Antarctica stores so much of Earth's freshwater, scientists are watching its frozen banks intently. Currently, only two areas of the continent show clear climate-related trends. One is the Antarctic Peninsula, where large-scale melting is occurring. The other is in the atmosphere, high above the tallest mainland mountain peaks. There, the annual return of the ozone hole is a worrisome reminder of environmental threats.

WHAT IF THE ICE MELTS?

Much confusion surrounds concerns about global warming and the melting of Earth's polar ice, especially Antarctic ice. Melting of ice shelves would have little direct impact on sea levels, because ice shelves are floating in the ocean. The volume of water they already displace would be equal to the volume of water that would result if they melted. The same is true of icebergs, pack ice, and Arctic ice, which are already free-floating. However, the destruction of Antarctica's ice shelves allows inland ice sheets to flow more quickly and freely to the sea. This "new ice" would displace water and cause sea levels to rise.

In theory, a total melting of the Antarctic ice sheets would raise sea levels about 200 feet (60 m). Such an increase would result in coastal flooding on a global scale. Many of the world's cities and islands also would disappear beneath the rising oceans. Fortunately, the likelihood of this happening is remote. Because it is so cold in the south polar region, melting of the Antarctic ice sheets would require a global temperature increase far in excess of the temperature increases that are currently forecast. In addition, if all this ice were to melt, the process would take hundreds, if not thousands, of years. This knowledge should not, however, downplay the impact that smaller-scale increases in sea levels would have on coastal areas and islands. Although scientists lack certainty about many of the factors related to global warming, most evidence indicates that global warming is likely to affect Antarctica. The projected effects of global warming on temperatures, sea levels, surface vegetation, and human populations are dire enough to warrant concern from everyone.

Antarctica's pack ice can extend between 1 million and 7.3 million square miles (1.6 million–11.7 million sq km), depending on the season.

In September 2001, the ozone hole over Antarctica was at its largest for that year—16,155,650 square miles (26,000,000 sq km). Similar in size to the springtime ozone holes of the previous three years, some researchers predict that the size of the ozone hole may begin to slowly decrease over the next 30 to 50 years, as chlorine levels in Earth's atmosphere decline.

In the image shown here, dark blue represents the thinnest levels of ozone, while yellow indicates the thickest ozone.

KEY CONCEPTS

Kyoto Protocol This international agreement was formally adopted by 84 countries in Kyoto, Japan, in 1997. It requires industrialized countries to reduce their greenhouse gas emissions by 2012. The U.S. has not yet ratified the agreement. In 2001, the U.S. renounced the treaty on the grounds of cost. As of 2002, the Kyoto Protocol's future is far from assured as various nations, following America's lead, have shown hesitation due to perceived negative effects on their respective economies.

Ozone Ozone is a naturally occurring molecule made up of three oxygen atoms bonded together. Ozone is formed from lightning strikes and the sun's high-energy ultraviolet (UV) radiation. At ground level, ozone is a toxic gas. The smell in the air after a thunderstorm is the odor of ozone. In the stratosphere, high above the ground, ozone is vital to life. It shields Earth's surface from overexposure to UV radiation. UV radiation can cause severe burns to the skin. It also damages the deoxyribonucleic acid (DNA) in living tissues, leading to cancers.

Ozone and the international community The United Nations Environment Programme has been assessing the ozone issue since 1977. In 1985, the Vienna Convention was convened to initiate an international agreement to protect the ozone layer and to increase scientific understanding of it. This led, in 1997, to the Montreal Protocol on Substances that Deplete the Ozone Layer. Four amendments to the protocol further strengthened its control mechanisms. In accordance with the protocol, September 16 of each year is proclaimed an International Day for the Preservation of the Ozone Layer.

Economics and the Environment

Oil and natural gas exist off Antarctica's shores. Valuable minerals such as gold, nickel, and platinum can be found on the mainland. Mining of these resources would damage or destroy the fragile Antarctic environment. The Environmental Protocol has addressed this concern. It has banned all mining activity in the region until 2048, at which point the ban may be reviewed.

Large-scale commercial fishing in the Antarctic region began in the 1970s. By the early 1980s, stocks of commercially desirable fish, such as Antarctic cod, were depleted. The Patagonian toothfish, an alternative commercially viable species, was also severely overfished. Longline hooks used to catch toothfish often snared seabirds such as albatrosses. Two albatross species are now endangered as a result.

Though the Convention on the Conservation of Antarctic Marine Living Resources (CCAMLR) has helped restore stocks of some species, overfishing remains a problem. IUU (illegal, unregulated, and unreported) fishing of toothfish is especially troubling. Catches that far exceed quotas threaten these over-stressed fish stocks. IUU fishing also continues to kill high numbers of seabirds.

The CCAMLR refers to IUU fishing as its most pressing problem. The agency launched a Catch Documentation Scheme in 2000. It now monitors global trade in and fishing of toothfish, and forces fishers to account for their actions. The scheme requires cooperation from nations that have fishing interests in the region. Time will tell how successful this scheme will be.

The most recent contributor to the Antarctic economy is tourism. Few places on Earth are so remote and unspoiled.

Without international interest and concern, Antarctic wildlife, such as this humpback whale, might not be around for long.

GUIDANCE FOR VISITORS TO THE ANTARCTIC

According to guidelines set out in the Antarctic Treaty, all visitors to Antarctica are expected to comply with the following:

- Unless one has a permit issued by a national authority, taking or interfering with Antarctic wildlife is prohibited.

- Because of their scientific, ecological, or historic value, entry into certain areas may be prohibited except in accordance with a permit issued by an appropriate national authority.

- Scientific research, facilities, and equipment must not be interfered with.

- Visitors must be prepared for severe and changeable weather. Clothing and equipment must meet Antarctic standards. Visitors must be aware of the fact that Antarctica is an inhospitable, unpredictable, and potentially dangerous place.

- Visitors should ensure that Antarctica remains relatively unaffected by human use and actions. It is important that the world's largest wilderness area stays that way.

Most tourists begin their Antarctic vacations in South America, where they board cruise ships that take them to their exotic destination. "Adventure" trips involving climbing and kayaking are also becoming popular.

Since tourism began in earnest in the 1980s, increasing numbers of people have been going ashore. The 1999/2000 tourist season was the most successful to date. About 15,000 people came to view the scenery, wildlife, and historic sites. Numbers dropped by several thousand between 2000 and 2002. Nevertheless, tourism is viewed as a growing industry, having seen a significant overall increase throughout the 1990s.

Most tourists arrive on cruise ships, although yachts have also appeared in recent years. Many factors affect the expense of a vacation "on the Ice." Costs generally range from as low as $3,000 to $15,000 or more.

Another "cost" of tourism is the possibility of environmental damage. Fortunately, the Environmental Protocol also applies to tourists. The International Association of Antarctic Tour Operators (IAATO) requires compliance with the spirit and letter of the protocol. Thus, visitors must not disturb wildlife in any way. Visitors also cannot smoke, leave litter, or wander into protected areas. Research stations are also restricted areas.

TOURIST TRENDS IN ANTARCTICA

How Many Tourists?

The number of tourists visiting Antarctica climbed steadily throughout the 1990s. Despite a drop in numbers after 2000, tourism is projected to increase in the future.

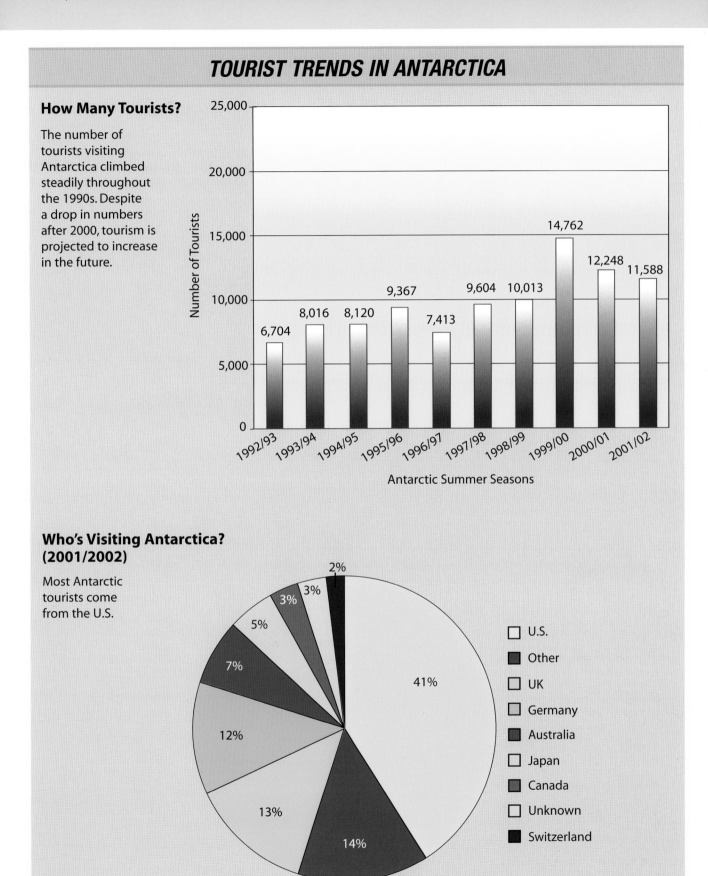

Number of Tourists

- 1992/93: 6,704
- 1993/94: 8,016
- 1994/95: 8,120
- 1995/96: 9,367
- 1996/97: 7,413
- 1997/98: 9,604
- 1998/99: 10,013
- 1999/00: 14,762
- 2000/01: 12,248
- 2001/02: 11,588

Antarctic Summer Seasons

Who's Visiting Antarctica? (2001/2002)

Most Antarctic tourists come from the U.S.

- U.S. 41%
- Other 14%
- UK 13%
- Germany 12%
- Australia 7%
- Japan 5%
- Canada 3%
- Unknown 3%
- Switzerland 2%

Tourists and environmental groups were the first to focus attention on pollution problems in Antarctica.

KEY CONCEPTS

Mining economics The Environmental Protocol notwithstanding, commercial mining in Antarctica may not be economically viable. Mining in the region would not only have to be technically feasible, it would have to be profitable as well. High production costs would require the use of a huge industrial plant for large deposits and would play havoc with the Antarctic environment. The prospect of such development roused "green" groups into action all over the world in the early 1980s. The notion of Antarctica as a world park, an idea first suggested by New Zealand and fiercely supported by Greenpeace, dates from this period.

Oil and gas In 1973, the U.S. experimental drill ship *Glomar Challenger* discovered gaseous hydrocarbons when drilling in the Ross Sea. Further investigations showed that the continental shelf of Antarctica likely contained large deposits of oil and gas. Mining on the ice-covered mainland would have meant crossing new frontiers of technology, and would have been extremely expensive. In contrast, offshore drilling for oil, even at depths of 1,600 feet (490 m) or more, was within the realm of possibility.

Duties: Studies the physical aspects and dynamics of Earth

Education: Bachelor of Science degree in geology

Interests: Science, rocks, and minerals, and working in the outdoors

For further information on a career in geology, head to **www.geol.lsu. edu/department/note-about. html** or **www.earthscienceworld. org/careers**

Careers in Focus

Geologists study the history and physical aspects of Earth. As a result of examining rocks, minerals, and fossils, they are able to learn much about our planet, from how it was formed and what it would have looked like millions of years ago, to where valuable oil, minerals, natural gas deposits, and underground water are to be found.

Geologists are becoming more involved in studying, preserving, and cleaning up the environment. These geological scientists may design and monitor waste disposal sites, and locate safe sites for hazardous waste disposal. Geological scientists also preserve water resources and clean up contaminated land.

Geologists may specialize in a wide variety of fields. Geological oceanographers study the ocean floor, using **remote sensing** to collect data. Paleontologists examine fossils to better understand the evolution of Earth's flora and fauna, and the processes that have made our planet what it is today. Hydrogeologists analyze underground and surface water in order to determine its distribution and properties.

Petroleum geologists use sophisticated instruments and computers to map, locate, and study oil and gas deposits. Seismologists apply their knowledge to detect earthquakes. Many geologists use their knowledge to understand and solve environmental issues.

With such a variety of branches, geologists find themselves working in many different environments and capacities, and with widely different aims. Many work mainly in laboratories or offices, while others may be required to spend a great deal of time outdoors, often in relatively inaccessible places.

The Antarctic Treaty System

By the 1940s, seven countries had laid claim to parts of Antarctica. The Antarctic Peninsula was a particular source of heated debate. Britain, Argentina, and Chile all had overlapping claims in this area. Diplomats were looking for new ways to settle such disputes. The solution came, fittingly, from the realm of science.

In most respects, Antarctica has always been a place for scientists, not soldiers. The International Geophysical Year of 1957/1958 provided an important model of scientific cooperation. During this time, scientists from many nations successfully collaborated on an Antarctic research program. The idea that Antarctica should be preserved for peace and science took root. Encouraged by the United States, the international community agreed to suspend their territorial claims. The Antarctic Treaty is the formal declaration of this agreement. Signed in Washington, D.C., on December 1, 1959, the treaty came into effect in 1961. It remains one of the most effective international agreements ever reached.

Over its history, the Antarctic Treaty has been reinforced by other agreements. The Environmental Protocol is the most recent example. As well, other agencies have been

Many people have their photograph taken at the ceremonial South Pole. The geographic South Pole is about 295 feet (90 m) away.

ANTARCTIC TREATY CONSULTATIVE PARTIES (27)

Claimants (7)	Non-Claimants (20)		
*Argentina	Belgium	Germany	*South Africa
*Australia	Brazil	India	South Korea
*Chile	Bulgaria	Italy	Spain
*France	China	*Japan	Sweden
*New Zealand	Ecuador	The Netherlands	*USA
*Norway	Finland	Peru	Uruguay
*UK		Poland	
		*Russia	

(*original signers of Antarctic Treaty)

(*original signers of Antarctic Treaty)

ANTARCTIC TREATY NON-CONSULTATIVE PARTIES (18)

Austria	Estonia	Romania
Canada	Greece	Slovak Republic
Colombia	Guatemala	Switzerland
Cuba	Hungary	Turkey
Czech Republic	North Korea	Ukraine
Denmark	Papua New Guinea	Venezuela

established to help treaty parties conduct their work. The Scientific Committee on Antarctic Research (SCAR) is an unofficial coordinating body. The Council of Managers of National Antarctic Programs (COMNAP) is made up of managers from national agencies that oversee scientific operations. Independent international agencies, such as the United Nations (UN), the World Meteorological Organization, and the International Union for the Conservation of Nature, also provide expert advice.

Along with the Antarctic Treaty itself, these agreements and organizations make up the Antarctic Treaty System. Parties belonging to the treaty system include both Consultative parties and Non-Consultative Parties. By 2002, there were 45 parties altogether, representing about 80 percent of Earth's population. Large countries that are not currently party to the treaty include Indonesia, Pakistan, Mexico, and Iran.

Despite continued measures to ensure conservation of the environment, Antarctica remains the subject of ongoing scientific research and international discussion.

THE ANTARCTIC TREATY SYSTEM: RULES AND REGULATIONS

The Antarctic Treaty System consists of the 1959 treaty, the measures and recommendations arising from successive consultative meetings, and the conventions and protocols listed below. The system applies to all land and ice shelves below 60 °S, and to all marine life south of the Antarctic Convergence.

Agreed Measures for the Conservation of Antarctic Fauna and Flora (1964)

Convention for the Conservation of Antarctic Seals (1972)

Convention on the Conservation of Antarctic Marine Living Resources (1980)

Convention on the Regulation of Antarctic Mineral Resource Activities (1988, but superseded by the Environmental Protocol)

Protocol on Environmental Protection to the Antarctic Treaty (the Madrid, or Environmental, Protocol—1991)

The International Whaling Commission (IWC) works with the Antarctic Treaty System to protect Antarctica's whales.

KEY CONCEPTS

International Geophysical Year
This 1957/1958 period of scientific activity involved 67 countries working together to develop a better understanding of Earth and its place in the universe. On Antarctica, 12 nations established 45 research stations, paving the way for the Antarctic Treaty. Among their achievements were new theories about glaciers, a reliable estimate for the total volume of water stored in Antarctica's ice cap, and an improved understanding of weather patterns in the Southern Hemisphere.

Parties to the treaty
Consultative parties include the original seven territorial claimants, five other countries that supported the treaty from the outset, such as Japan and the United States, and other countries that have done substantial research in the Antarctic, such as Germany and Sweden. These parties have a right to vote at the regular meetings that are mandated under the treaty. Non-consultative parties are those countries that have agreed to abide by the treaty.

HIGHLIGHTS FROM THE ANTARCTIC TREATY

The following articles are paraphrased excerpts from the Antarctic Treaty:

Article I: (1) Antarctica will be used for peaceful purposes only. All military measures, such as the creation of military bases and fortifications, practice of military maneuvers, as well as weapons testing, will be prohibited. (2) Use of military personnel or equipment is permitted for scientific research or other peaceful purposes.

Article II: Nations will continue to practice scientific cooperation.

Article III: To maximize economy and efficiency of operations, information about scientific programs, scientific personnel, and scientific observations and results will be exchanged.

Article IV: The Treaty does not recognize existing territorial claims, nor does it prejudice such claims. No new claims can be asserted while the Treaty is in force.

Article V: Nuclear explosions and the disposal of radioactive waste will be prohibited.

Article VI: The conditions of the Treaty apply to the area south of 60 °South Latitude, including all ice shelves. Sea navigation rights remain subject to the Law of the Sea.

Article VII: Treaty-state observers have free access, including aerial observation, to any area. They may also inspect all stations, installations, and equipment. Advance notice must be given of any Antarctic expedition, occupation of research stations, and introduction of military personnel or equipment.

Articles VIII to XIV: Treaty states must hold periodic consultative meetings and discourage activities by any country contrary to the Treaty. Observers and scientists are under jurisdiction of their own states. Disputes are to be settled by the parties or the International Court of Justice. Any UN member nation may consent to the Treaty.

Time Line of Events

1772–1775
Captain James Cook becomes the first person to cross the Antarctic Circle.

Early 1800s
Widespread hunting of fur seals and elephant seals begins, continuing into the 1960s.

1820
American whaling captain and explorer Nathaniel Brown Palmer sees the Antarctic continent from near the tip of the Antarctic Peninsula.

1823
English explorer James Weddell sails further south than anyone previously, into the sea that today bears his name.

1840
The first deep-sea sounding to measure the sea bottom is undertaken by James Clark Ross.

1899
Norwegian explorer Carsten Borchgrevink and his crew become the first people to spend a winter on the Antarctic continent.

1904
Antarctic whaling becomes a global industry.

1911
Roald Amundsen and his party become the first people to reach the South Pole.

1912
Robert Falcon Scott and his party reach the South Pole, only to discover that Amundsen reached it first.

1929
U.S. Admiral Richard Byrd conducts the first airplane flight over the South Pole.

1933
Macquarie Island becomes a wildlife sanctuary.

1946
The U.S. Navy leads Operation Highjump, a large-scale exercise to provide troops with experience in polar environmental conditions.

1956
Construction begins on the first South Pole Station.

1957–1958
The International Geophysical Year unifies scientists and scientific endeavors across the globe, laying the groundwork for the Antarctic Treaty.

1959
The Antarctic Treaty is signed in Washington, D.C., by 12 countries.

1961
The Antarctic Treaty comes into effect.

1969
Swedish-American Lars-Eric Lindblad designs the *Lindblad Explorer*, a cruise ship designed to carry tourists to the continent. This marks the beginning of Antarctica's tourism industry.

1972
A convention for the protection of Antarctic seals is established.

■■■ **The dome at the Amundsen-Scott South Pole Station was completed in 1975. It replaced the original South Pole station. A third station is now being built.**

1973

The U.S. drill ship *Glamor Challenger* discovers gaseous hydrocarbons in the Ross Sea.

1979

An Air New Zealand DC-10, carrying 257 people, crashes into Mount Erebus, killing all on board.

1980

The Convention on the Conservation of Marine Living Resources is adopted as part of the Antarctic Treaty System.

1983

The world's lowest recorded air temperature is measured at Vostok Station, in East Antarctica.

1991

The Protocol on Environmental Protection is signed in Madrid.

1997

The Kyoto Protocol is adopted by 84 countries.

1998

The Environmental Protocol enters into force.

2001

Ann Bancroft and Liv Arnesen become the first women to cross the Antarctic mainland, on skis.

Concept Web

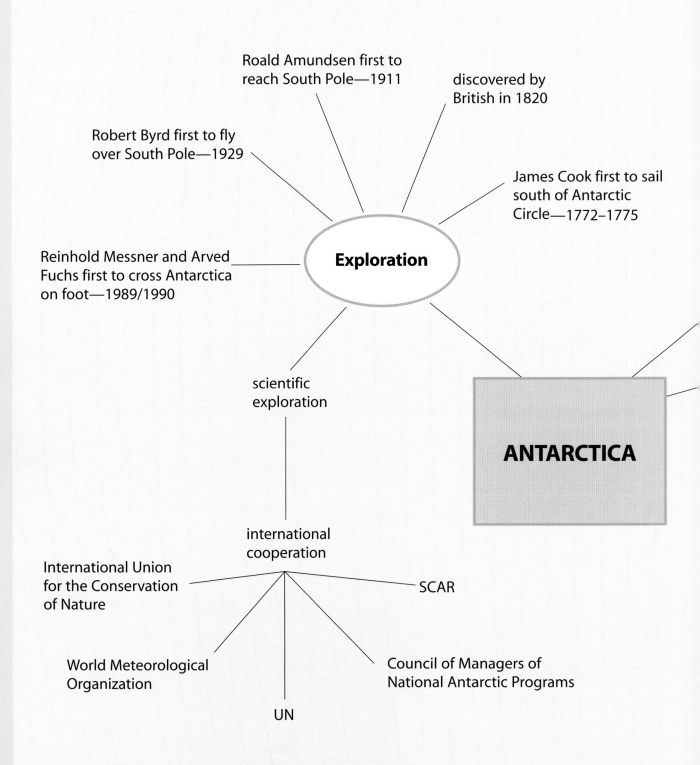

Roald Amundsen first to reach South Pole—1911

discovered by British in 1820

Robert Byrd first to fly over South Pole—1929

James Cook first to sail south of Antarctic Circle—1772–1775

Reinhold Messner and Arved Fuchs first to cross Antarctica on foot—1989/1990

Exploration

scientific exploration

ANTARCTICA

international cooperation

International Union for the Conservation of Nature

SCAR

World Meteorological Organization

Council of Managers of National Antarctic Programs

UN

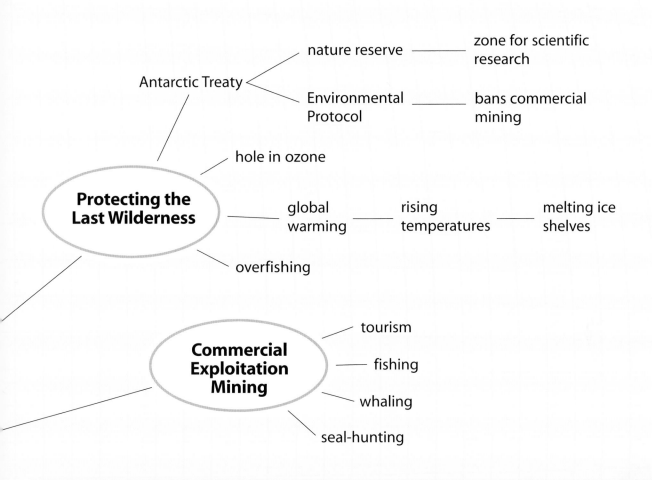

Antarctic Treaty
- nature reserve —— zone for scientific research
- Environmental Protocol —— bans commercial mining

Protecting the Last Wilderness
- hole in ozone
- global warming —— rising temperatures —— melting ice shelves
- overfishing

Commercial Exploitation Mining
- tourism
- fishing
- whaling
- seal-hunting

MAKE YOUR OWN CONCEPT WEB

A concept web is a useful summary tool. It can also be used to plan your research or help you write an essay or report. To make your own concept web, follow the steps below:

- You will need a large piece of unlined paper and a pencil.
- First, read through your source material, such as *Antarctica: The Last Wilderness* in the Understanding Global Issues series.
- Write the main idea, or concept, in large letters in the center of the page.
- On a sheet of lined paper, jot down all words, phrases, or lists that you know are connected with the concept. Try to do this from memory.
- Look at your list. Can you group your words and phrases in certain topics or themes? Connect the different topics with lines to the center, or to other "branches."
- Critique your concept web. Ask questions about the material on your concept web: Does it all make sense? Are all the links shown? Could there be other ways of looking at it? Is anything missing?
- What more do you need to find out? Develop questions for those areas you are still unsure about or where information is missing. Use these questions as a basis for further research.

Quiz

Multiple Choice

1. Which of the following statements about Antarctica is false?
   a) Antarctica is larger than the United States and Mexico combined.
   b) About two percent of the continental landmass is free of ice.
   c) Blizzards are common on the continent.
   d) Most research stations on Antarctica are military bases.

2. Excluding the coast, animal life on the continent does not include:
   a) insects
   b) plants
   c) mammals
   d) birds

3. The Antarctic Treaty was signed in:
   a) 1957
   b) 1959
   c) 1961
   d) 1958

4. Ice cores provide scientists with evidence that helps them better understand:
   a) global warming
   b) atmospheric carbon dioxide of the past and present
   c) prehistoric climatic conditions
   d) all of the above

5. Mining on Antarctica is prohibited because:
   a) the Antarctic Treaty forbids it
   b) the United Nations declared Antarctica a world park
   c) the Convention on the Conservation of Antarctic Marine Living Resources has shown that krill are becoming endangered
   d) the Environmental Protocol requires a suspension of mining interests in the region

6. A hole in Earth's ozone layer opens over Antarctica each spring. This is a concern because:
   a) ozone is a toxic gas
   b) ultraviolet radiation is causing global warming
   c) ultraviolet radiation causes cancers
   d) ozone destroys carbon dioxide

7. Tourism can benefit Antarctica economically. Environmentally, tourism can have a negative impact on the Antarctic environment because:
    a) it is extremely fragile
    b) penguins are unafraid of people
    c) people get in the way of research activities
    d) the Environmental Protocol did not include provisions for tourism

Where Did It Happen?

1. Robert Falcon Scott lost his life while traveling back from this place.
2. The largest U.S. research station is located here.
3. East and West Antarctica are separated by this feature.
4. The Antarctic Treaty was signed here.

True or False

1. Antarctica contains half of the world's water resources.
2. Seals and whales are not protected by the Convention on the Conservation of Antarctic Marine Living Resources (CCAMLR).
3. Krill are vital to Antarctic food webs.
4. Antarctica is considered the harshest, most hostile environment on Earth.

Answers on page 53

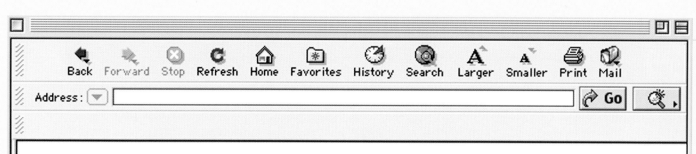

Internet Resources

The following Web sites provide more information on Antarctica:

Explore Antarctica
http://www.secretsoftheice.org/index.html
Experience life and work in Antarctica. Observe the continent's natural features, both past and present. Join in various scientific expeditions and pursue other pathways for learning about this most intriguing of continents. Some of the links on this Web site are "hidden" behind others, so be sure to explore all possible nooks and crannies.

Virtual Antarctica
http://www.doc.ic.ac.uk/~kpt/terraquest/va/
Visit the last continent from the safety and comfort of a computer monitor. Learn how an Antarctic expedition is mounted, or "hike" through one of the most unusual environments on Earth. Meet the different members of the expedition team, and pursue numerous other print and electronic resources to develop a better understanding of Antarctica.

Some Web sites stay current longer than others. To find other Antarctica Web sites, enter terms such as "Antarctica," "Antarctic Treaty," or "South Pole" into a search engine.

Further Reading

Amundsen, Roald E. *The South Pole: An Account of the Norwegian Antarctic Expedition in the Fram: 1910-1912*. New York: New York University Press, 2001.

Cherry-Garrard, Apsley. *The Worst Journey in the World*. New York: Carroll & Graf, 1997.

Loewen, Nancy, and Ann Bancroft. *Four to the Pole!* North Haven, CT: Linnet Books, 2001.

Mastro, Jim. *Antarctica: A Year at the Bottom of the World*. Boston: Bulfinch Press, 2002.

Rubin, Jeff. *Lonely Planet: Antarctica*. New York: Lonely Planet, 2000.

Scott, Robert Falcon, and Beryl Bainbridge. *Scott's Last Expedition: The Journals*. New York: Carroll & Graf, 1996.

Wheeler, Sara. *Terra Incognita: Travels in Antarctica*. New York: Modern Library, 1999.

Answers

Multiple Choice
1. d) 2. c) 3. b) 4. d) 5. d) 6. c) 7. a)

Where Did It Happen?
1. The South Pole 2. McMurdo Sound 3. Transantarctic Mountains 4. Washington, D.C.

True or False
1. F 2. T 3. T 4. T

Glossary

chlorofluorocarbons: the chemicals largely responsible for destroying ozone in the upper atmosphere

Cold War: term that refers to the tensions that developed between the U.S. and USSR from the end of World War II up until 1989

consensus: general agreement among the members of a group

continental shelves: the sloping area of a coastline that continues for a distance into the surrounding sea

convention: a binding agreement that has substantial power because it defines standards of conduct and behavior

ecosystem: a system formed by the interaction of plants and animals with the environment

escarpment: long, steep, cliff-like ridge of land or rock

fauna: the animal life in an area

flora: the plant life in an area

food webs: networks of feeding relationships among predators and their prey

indigenous: native to a region

invertebrates: animals lacking a backbone or spinal column

lichen: an organism comprised of two other organisms (an alga and a fungus) living together for the mutual benefit of each other

lubricating: applying a substance, such as oil or grease, to decrease friction

microbes: microorganisms, especially disease-causing bacteria

oceanographer: a scientist who studies the chemistry, geology, and biology of the oceans

ozone: a form of oxygen in Earth's upper atmosphere that absorbs and prevents harmful ultraviolet rays from reaching Earth's surface

physiology: the organic processes and functions in an organism and/or its parts

plate tectonics: theory based on the idea that the Earth's crust is made up of massive segments, or plates, whose movements are responsible for earthquakes, the formation of mountains, etc.

protocol: a treaty that amends or changes the terms of a previously existing treaty

remote sensing: gathering of information from a distance, using radar, aerial photography, and satellite imagery

treaty: a formal agreement among nations that clearly outlines their obligations to one another

Index

Photo Credits

Cover: Two emperor penguins on ice (**Ann Hawthorne/Arctic Photo**); **B&C Alexander:** pages 8/9, 16, 18/19; **Bancroft Arnesen Explore:** page 11; **CORBIS/MAGMA:** page 7 (**Bettmann**); **Corel Corporation:** pages 13, 14, 20, 45; **DigitalVision:** pages 2/3, 40, 44; **Paul Drummend/B&C Alexander:** pages 22/23; **Ann Hawthorne/B&C Alexander:** pages 24/25, 42, 47; **Landsat 7 Science Team & NASA GSFC:** page 32; **National Archives of Canada:** page 6; **National Science Foundation:** page 21 (**Mark Sabbatini**), 27 (**Melanie Conner**), 41 (**Josh Landis**); **NSF Office of Polar Programs:** page 26; **Cagan H. Sekercioglu:** pages 1, 4/5, 10, 15, 34, 36, 38; **Greg Shirah, GSFC Scientific Visualization Studio:** page 35.